Little Swan

by Adèle Geras

illustrated by Johanna Westerman

A STEPPING STONE BOOK

Random House New York

SISKIYOU CO. OFFICE OF ED
LIBRARY
609 S. GOLD ST., YREKA, CA 96097

Text copyright © 1995 by Adèle Geras
Illustrations copyright © 1995 by Johanna Westerman

All rights reserved under International and Pan-American Copyright Conventions.
Published in the United States by Random House, Inc., New York, and simultaneously
in Canada by Random House of Canada Limited, Toronto.

Based on the short story "Little Swan" by Adèle Geras,
which was published in *Prima Ballerina: A Book of Ballet Stories,*
edited by Miriam Hodgson, Methuen Children's Books, 1992.
Copyright © 1992 by Adèle Geras.

Library of Congress Cataloging-in-Publication Data
Geras, Adèle.
Little Swan / by Adèle Geras ; illustrated by Johanna Westerman.
p. cm.
"A Stepping stone book."
SUMMARY: Annie's seven-year-old sister Weezer begins taking ballet lessons, and Annie
watches as she becomes a "proper ballerina."
ISBN 0-679-87000-8 (pbk.) — ISBN 0-679-97000-2 (lib. bdg.)
[1. Ballet dancing—Fiction. 2. Sisters—Fiction.] I. Westerman, Johanna, ill. II. Title.
PZ7.G29354Li 1995
[Fic]—dc20
94-35024

Manufactured in the United States of America   10 9 8 7 6 5 4 3 2 1

LIBRARY

For Jacqueline Wilson

Chapter One

My name is Annie. I'm ten years old. Weezer, my little sister, is seven. Her real name is Louisa, but nobody calls her that. About six months ago, she started nagging our mother. Weezer is an excellent nagger. She never stops. She wanted to go to ballet classes. So at every meal, she tried a different kind of nagging.

"Some of my friends started going in first grade." (That was one kind.)

"It's not very expensive." (That was another.)

"St. Christopher's Hall is so close. I could walk there by myself." (That was a third.)

We were in the middle of breakfast. Mom said, "No, you couldn't. You have to cross three main roads. You know you're always in a dream."

"Annie'll take me," said Weezer. She smiled at me. "You will, won't you, Annie."

"I guess I will," I answered. It's best to agree with Weezer. She can stay in a terrible mood for days and days if you don't. Once, her friends Tricia and Maisie were playing Kings and Queens. Weezer wanted to be the queen, but the others decided she should be the princess.

"It was my turn," she told me. "I was princess last time." She sulked about it for three days, and in the end Maisie said she didn't mind being princess for the next four games, and Weezer could be queen if she liked.

Mom must have realized that Weezer was never going to stop nagging. She sighed.

"Okay," she said. "I give in. You can start next week. We'll have to buy everything you need."

Weezer's smile beamed out over the table. "I've got a list," she said. "I'll go get it."

"Finish your toast first," Mom said. But she was too late. Weezer had rushed out of the room. We could hear her clattering up the stairs. I ate the piece of buttered toast she'd left behind. I knew she wouldn't eat it now. Her dream was about to come true. I couldn't believe my bratty little sister was about to become a ballet dancer.

Weezer laid all her new equipment out on the bed.

"Look, Annie," she said. "Isn't it lovely?" I looked. I saw two pink leotards, two pairs of pink ballet slippers, a white cardigan, and a small pink suitcase. This suitcase had a picture on the lid. It was painted in gold and showed a ballerina standing on her points.

"Very nice," I said. I didn't think the stuff was anything to get excited about. But Weezer had other ideas. She was determined to make me see how wonderful each item was.

"These shoes are real leather, Annie. Feel how soft they are. They're real ballet shoes, even though they're not toe shoes. You aren't allowed to go on your points. Not till you're twelve. But the ribbons are satin. There's a special way to tie them. And I have to have my hair done up in a net. Did you see my hair net, Annie?"

"No," I said. "I missed that."

"This is it. And this is my cardigan. It crosses

over and ties in back." She started jumping up
and down.

"Lovely," I said. "But why is everything spread
out on the bed?"

"I'm going to pack my case," said Weezer.
"Isn't it a beautiful case? Don't you like this ballerina on the lid? I'm going to look just like this
when I grow up."

"I hope you won't be gold all over."

Weezer threw her hairbrush at me. She's a good thrower. It's time she learned when I'm kidding.

At last, the day came. In case we had forgotten, Weezer reminded us.

"It's the first class today," she said. She put a spoonful of dry cereal into her mouth. She was so excited she'd forgotten all about milk.

I passed the carton to her and said, "We're not going till four o'clock. Your pink suitcase is by the front door already."

"I put it there last night," said Weezer, "in case I forgot this morning."

"Have you remembered to pack everything?" Mom asked.

"Yes," said Weezer. "I checked my list."

I sighed. Perhaps now that Weezer was starting classes, we could take down the list she'd put up in our bedroom. She'd stuck it on the dressing-table mirror—right in the middle so that you couldn't see your whole face at once. After a few days, I knew that list by heart.

> Leotard
> Shoes
> Cardigan
> Hair net
> Brush and comb
> Hairpins
> Talcum powder

Everything was now safely shut up in the suitcase.

"Don't be late home from school today, Annie," said Weezer. "Remember you're taking me. We have to leave at four o'clock exactly."

"I know," I said. "You've told me. I won't be late. Promise."

I wasn't late, but Weezer made me drink my milk at top speed. She'd changed her mind. We would leave, she told me, at ten to four.

"We'll be early," I said. "And I want a cookie."

"The traffic may be very busy. There might be an accident. We might have to go the long way around." Weezer has a very vivid imagination. I swallowed the last drop of milk and took a cookie to eat on the way. Sometimes, I just had to listen to Weezer. She would just walk out of the house on her own if I wasn't ready.

There are twenty girls and five boys in the junior ballet class. The teacher, Miss Matting, is a thin, pale woman with a lot of blond hair done up in a bun on top of her head. One whole wall of the room is a mirror. All the children lined up at the barre along this wall for their exercises. I sat on a bench and watched.

Weezer stood between two girls from her class at school. I never realized how much she already knew about ballet. She knew the five foot positions and a few of the basic exercises. I had seen Tricia and Maisie teaching her on the playground. Also, for her last birthday, Mom had given her a book full of beautiful photographs of ballerinas and Weezer had looked at it very carefully every day. Miss Matting brought her out to the front to teach her how to curtsy properly.

"That's good," she said when Weezer had curtsied perfectly. "You're naturally very graceful. I'm sure you'll do well at ballet." Weezer's face was pink with pleasure. She looked at me, to make sure I'd heard. Tricia and Maisie looked proud that she'd done so well. Perhaps they'd been teaching her curtsies at school along with all the other things.

I heard one of the other girls whispering to her friend, "I bet she was at another class before she came here." I felt proud of Weezer too.

While the class continued, I looked around the room. It has a very high ceiling and lots of long, narrow windows. The floor is made of polished wood. There is an upright piano in one corner, and the pianist is a plump, elderly lady who kept her hat on all through the class. The bunch of cherries she had pinned to it jumped about as she nodded her head in time to the music. Later on, Weezer told me her name is Mrs. Standish.

At the end of the lesson, Miss Matting said, "Please sit down, children. I have an important announcement to make. We must start thinking about our annual show. We're going to do some very interesting dances this year. I shall be watching you all closely, and in a few weeks' time we will have auditions. Of course, everyone will have a chance to take part in the show, but there is a special dance we're going to do this year. I shall need four girl soloists. I'm sure you'll all try to do your best."

I glanced at Weezer. Her eyes were as wide open as they could be, and her mouth was open too. This was exactly the kind of competition that my sister loves, and I just knew that she'd already set her heart on being one of the chosen four.

Chapter Two

After the class, Weezer almost flew over the sidewalk. She was swinging her pink suitcase backward and forward.

"Oh, Annie," she said. "It was cool. Wasn't it cool? And there's going to be a show! A real show! I wish it was next week. Hurry up! I have to practice after supper. Come on!"

Weezer was walking so fast that she nearly knocked over one of our neighbors, Mrs. Posnansky. She is a thin, small woman who wears her gray hair in a bun. Her dresses are mostly black, but you can tell she loves pretty scarves and lace collars and long necklaces. She was walking out of someone's driveway and Weezer only just missed her.

"Oh, Mrs. Posnansky," she cried. "I'm sorry. I didn't mean to scare you."

Mrs. Posnansky smiled. "You are hurricane. You are not girl."

"I've been to my first ballet class," said Weezer. "I'm so excited. I feel like running and running. I don't think I'll ever sit down again."

"Aah!" sighed Mrs. Posnansky. "The ballet! How beautiful is it! How I love! In Russia, of course—"

Weezer interrupted her. "I'm sorry, Mrs. Posnansky, I have to go now."

"Of course, of course," said Mrs. Posnansky. "Your mother waits to hear all about class. I tell you stories from Russia on other day."

She set off across the street. Her house was just opposite ours. At her door, she turned and waved. Weezer had already rushed inside our house, but I waved back at Mrs. Posnansky.

Later I said to Weezer, "You should listen to Mrs. Posnansky. She was born in Russia. Lots of famous dancers come from there. Maybe she knew one of them."

"I bet she didn't," said Weezer. "Anyway, I can't listen to her. We hardly know her at all. We've never even been in her house." She disappeared upstairs to do exercises in front of the mirror, and I thought about how much fun it would be to visit Mrs. Posnansky. I like seeing

how people decorate their homes, and Mrs. Posnansky's was sure to be full of interesting things
to look at.

Weezer has wanted to be a ballet dancer ever
since she was four years old. That Christmas,
Mom and Dad took us to see *The Nutcracker*. I
had a book with the story in it, and I'd read it to
Weezer over and over again. She knew it by
heart. She was longing to see Clara, the little girl
who is given a gift of a magic Nutcracker that
turns into a prince. She couldn't wait to see the
snowflakes, the flowers, and the Sugar Plum
Fairy.

On the day of the performance, Weezer woke
up at six a.m. and pulled me out of bed. She
wanted to put on her party dress right away and
said that I had to help her. Then she made me
braid her hair.

"We're not going till nighttime," I said. I was
cold and mad and sleepy.

"Don't care," said Weezer, pushing out her
bottom lip. "Want it now!" Weezer said that a lot
when she was small: "Want it now!" Dad used to
kid her about it all the time.

Dad was living with us then. He doesn't live here any more. He and Mom are divorced.

"Annie," he'd said to me, "you're the grown-up one. Will you help me tell Weezer? Mom and I feel we'd be happier living apart, but we both still love you very, very much. And I'll still see you. Even though I'm moving away, I'm still your Dad. I'll always be your Dad. Do you understand that?"

"Yes," I said. "I understand." I didn't really, but I could see Dad was sad. I wanted him to look happier.

"And will you help me tell Weezer?"

"Yes," I said. Telling Weezer wasn't easy. At first, she pretended she didn't know what we meant. When Dad left, she cried and cried.

"Don't cry," I said, over and over again. "Dad loves us very much."

Weezer's face turned red with fury. "No, he does not! He doesn't love us enough. He'd stay here if he did." I couldn't think of anything to say to that.

In the end, we all got used to it. We see Dad on weekends sometimes, and during vacations.

We speak to him on the phone a lot, but everything is different now that he's gone.

Dad was still living with us when we went to see *The Nutcracker*. After he left, Weezer talked about that evening all the time.

"Curtains," she'd say. "Remember the red curtains?"

"Yes," I'd answer.

"Draw me the Sugar Plum Fairy," she'd say. I did the best I could. Weezer started twirling about in front of the mirror. She pointed her toes. She walked about on tiptoe. She took our nutcracker out of the kitchen drawer and wrapped it in a napkin. She carried it everywhere. She began to keep a scrapbook, and we all looked out for photos of ballet dancers. When we found them, in magazines or newspapers, she would cut them out and paste them in. If there was a ballet on TV, Weezer would be sitting in front of the set fifteen minutes before it started.

By the time she began nagging Mom about classes, Weezer had been crazy about ballet for years.

 *Chapter Three*

For the next three Tuesdays, Weezer went to her class after school. When she wasn't at class, she practiced and practiced.

"I've worked real hard at everything," she told me.

"I know," I said. I'd even seen her using the school railings as a barre during lunch break. Almost every day Tricia and Maisie came to our house. First they would turn our living room into another studio. Then they'd spend hours at the kitchen table discussing Miss Matting's special dance. What could she be planning this year?

"My sister went to Miss Matting's," said Maisie. "They did a Sailors' Hornpipe. They had blue pleated skirts, and little hats with pom-poms on them."

"Maybe we'll be flowers," Tricia said.

"What about snowflakes?" Weezer suggested.

"Maybe," Maisie and Tricia nodded. "She does keep telling us how light we must be."

"Well," Weezer said, "we always have to be light. You can't have heavy ballet dancers."

"Maisie'll be heavy," said Tricia, "if she goes on eating so many cookies."

Maisie blushed. "I only had four...they're very small."

"Never mind that," said Weezer impatiently. "Finish up and we'll go and practice some more." She left the table and ran back to the living room. Maisie and Tricia followed her obediently.

When the day of the auditions came, Weezer was very quiet. All the way to St. Christopher's Hall she hardly said a word. She wasn't swinging her pink suitcase. She just walked along next to me, dragging her feet.

"What's the matter, Weezer?" I said. "Don't you feel well?"

"I feel funny," said Weezer. "I feel kind of fluttery inside. But I'm not ill."

"Butterflies in your stomach," I said. Weezer

giggled. "I guess you're nervous. Are you?"

"No, I'm not," said Weezer. Then she paused. "Yes, I am nervous. What if..." Her voice faded away.

"What if what?" I asked. "Come on, Weezer. At least speak properly."

Weezer looked down at her feet. "What if I'm not chosen? For the special dance. What if Maisie and Tricia are and I'm not? What then?"

"Then you'll be in the chorus," I said. "There's nothing wrong with that. You only just started. Maybe you'll be chosen next time. It wouldn't be the end of the world, Weezer."

Weezer snorted at me. "You don't say 'chorus' in ballet," she said. "You say 'corps de ballet.'"

I could tell just by looking at her that she thought not being chosen would be the most dreadful thing that could ever happen to her.

After a few exercises, all the children sat down on the floor. Miss Matting said: "I can see you are all as jittery as can be. I know why. You all want to be chosen as soloists. You're all nervous. I know you are all going to dance as well as you can, but I'd just like to say one thing. In ballet, what matters is the whole dance, not just certain people's parts. The corps de ballet is just as vital as the most famous ballerina. Real professional dancers try as hard as they can, no matter what they are dancing. Please, all of you, remember this: If you are not chosen this time, you may be chosen next time. I am proud of all of you. Just do your very best."

Everyone was smiling, except Weezer. She wanted to be chosen. Nothing I said, and nothing Miss Matting said, made any difference at all.

"Now, children," said Miss Matting. "This is the sequence I want you to learn. It's very short."

For fifteen minutes, everyone practiced running, jumping, and twirling in the way Miss Matting had shown them. Then they started to dance the short sequence one at a time. Miss Matting sat on a chair with a clipboard and scribbled on a sheet of paper.

Then Miss Matting had just the girls come to the front of the class, one by one, to do a few steps. I watched closely. They all looked very much the same. When it came to Weezer's turn, though, *I* was the one with butterflies in my stomach. I couldn't look. I squeezed my eyes

shut and said to myself: Please, please, let Weezer do well. Let her be chosen. By the time I'd opened my eyes, Weezer had sat down again, and someone else was dancing.

It took a long time for all the girls to do their dance.

"Thank you very much, everyone," Miss Matting said at the end. "I'm sure you're all anxious to know who's been picked, so I shall stop the class now and allow you to get dressed. When you're ready, come in here and sit down quietly. I shall tell you all about the dance we'll be doing, and give you the names of the four soloists."

Usually, Weezer was very slow to change out of her leotard and into her clothes. Today she was back in the hall in a couple of minutes. She sat down next to Tricia and Maisie. She was staring very hard at the floor, and clutching her little suitcase so hard her knuckles were white. Miss Matting clapped her hands for attention.

"Now, children, the first thing I'd like to say is how proud I am of all of you. You did very well.

"I've decided, this year, to do something truly exciting. We will be dancing to Tchaikovsky's lovely music for *Swan Lake*. The boys will do a snowmen's dance and the girls will be a corps de ballet of swan maidens. The four girls I've chosen will dance a version of the Dance of the Little Swans that I've choreographed." Every eye in the class was on Miss Matting. Some people had their mouths open. Weezer was biting her lip.

"These, then," said Miss Matting, "are the four names..."

 *Chapter Four*

"...Marion Wolfson, Louisa Blair, Janet Gregory, and Dolores Delano."

Weezer blinked. Just for a split second, she didn't recognize her name.

"Louisa Blair—that's me!" she said to Tricia. "I've been chosen! Oh, Tricia, I wish you and Maisie had been chosen too!"

Miss Matting was still speaking. "Of course, the Little Swans need understudies. Imagine if all our soloists wake up on the morning of the show covered in measles. So Maisie Fellowes, Tricia Little, Sharon Goodbody, and Elizabeth Reynolds will also learn the steps." That seemed to make everyone very happy. Weezer and Tricia and Maisie did a little war dance together.

All the way home, Weezer kept saying, "I'm a

Little Swan, Annie! I'm going to be in a special dance. A Little Swan! Wait till I tell Mom!"

We talked about nothing else at supper.

"I'm so glad Tricia and Maisie are understudies," Weezer said. "It means we can practice together. And Annie, guess what? Tricia's mom says she can take me to class in the car each week. She can bring me back, too. You won't have to walk with me anymore. Isn't that great?"

"I guess," I said. I should have been happy, but I felt quite sad. I'd enjoyed taking Weezer to her ballet class. I liked the cloakroom, which smelled of talcum powder. I liked seeing what color leotard Miss Matting was wearing. I imagined her closet full of hundreds of different dance outfits.

"I must phone Dad," Weezer said, "and tell him about being a Little Swan."

"Cygnet," I said. "The proper word for a little swan is a cygnet. The dance should be called the Dance of the Cygnets."

"But it isn't!" Weezer was beginning to look dangerously pink. "It's called the Dance of the Little Swans. Ask anybody. Anybody who knows anything about ballet. Tchaikovsky could have called it whatever he liked. He chose Little Swans. So there." Weezer began stabbing the ice cream in her bowl.

"Okay," I said. "Okay. Little Swans it is." I didn't dare to tell her that Tchaikovsky probably called the dance something in Russian. She would have thrown her ice cream at me.

After supper, Weezer phoned Dad. I heard only her part of the conversation.

Some of it went like this: "Will you try? I really, really want you to see me being a Little Swan. I'm going to get you a ticket. Then if you are here, you'll be allowed in...Okay...but promise you'll try. Bye, Dad."

When I got on the phone, Dad said, "Annie, I don't think I can make it to Weezer's show. I did try to tell her, but you know Weezer. She sets her heart on something. Then she won't take no for an answer. Will you try to explain? Please? In the next few weeks, just try and get it into her head. I probably won't be there."

"But you will try?" I said. "If I get Weezer to understand, will you try?"

"Of course I will, Annie. You know that. But I'd hate to promise Weezer something and then disappoint her."

"Right," I said. "I'll do my best, Dad."

I was used to being the one who had to explain things to my little sister. I just hoped she wouldn't blame me if Dad didn't come to the show.

There were a lot of rehearsals over the next couple of weeks. Tricia's mom picked Weezer up and took her to classes. She also took her to extra rehearsals for the Little Swans and their understudies. That wasn't enough for Weezer. She was a Little Swan at home. She was a Little Swan at school. She was a Little Swan every minute of the day. She had a cassette tape with the *Swan Lake* music on it. Whenever Tricia and Maisie came to our house, she put it on. Then all three girls twirled around our dining room, giggling loudly. The Little Swan tune was beginning to get on my nerves.

One Saturday afternoon, Weezer came into the kitchen with a big grin all over her face.

"Guess what?" she said.

"What?"

"I just helped Mrs. Posnansky carry her groceries home."

Mom, who was sitting at the kitchen table said, "That doesn't sound like you, Weezer. How did that happen?"

"Well," said Weezer, "I was just looking out of the bedroom window and I saw old Mrs. Posnansky coming down the street carrying a big bag of groceries. So I went out to help her."

"But," I said, "she must have been nearly home by the time you got to her."

Weezer glared at me, and was just opening her mouth to answer, when Mom said soothingly, "Every little bit helps, Weezer. It was a very kind thing for you to have done."

Weezer smiled and said to me, "You just wish you could have been there, that's all. We had a real conversation. Mrs. Posnansky is a very interesting person. She comes all the way from Russia."

"We knew that," I said. "Long ago."

"I know, but she told me all about it. She told me about the Russian ballet, and a special school that young dancers can go to in St. Petersburg. And she asked me about my classes. I told her I was going to be a Little Swan. She was very impressed. I remember exactly what she said.

Every word. She said: 'You are real ballet dancer. This I see very clear.'"

"Did you go into her house?"

"No," said Weezer, rather sadly. "She asked me to, but I said I couldn't really, because Mom didn't even know I'd gone down the street to help her with the groceries. If she asks me another day, is it okay to go?"

"Sure," said Mom. "I hope you do have a chance to help her out again."

For a couple of days after that, Weezer kept looking out of the bedroom window for Mrs. Posnansky. But she never saw her, and in the end she finally gave up.

Chapter Five

One day at breakfast, there was a letter next to Weezer's plate.

"It's from Dad," she said. "Probably it's to say when he's getting here."

The show was only a few days away. Three blue tickets were pinned to the bulletin board in the kitchen.

For the past couple of weeks, I'd been trying to tell Weezer that the chances of Dad flying across the country to watch her being a Little Swan were very small.

"He'll want to see me dance," she'd kept saying. "He won't want to miss it."

"He won't have to," I said. "You know Miss Matting will put the whole show on video. She'll lend it to us when he's here. Then he can see you."

"It's not the same" was Weezer's answer. "It's not like watching it live."

"But it's nearly the same," I said. "You might have to settle for that."

Now Weezer was turning Dad's letter over and over in her hand.

"Open it, honey," Mom said, "and tell us what's in it."

Weezer opened the letter. She read it. She turned very pink. Then she turned very white. Then she gave a little howl and ran out of the room.

"Oh, my goodness," said Mom. "I told her not to get her hopes up."

"Me too," I said. "I kept telling her. She wouldn't listen. She only listens to things she likes hearing. I'll go talk to her. What does Dad say in the letter?"

"He says, 'Although I won't be there, I know you'll be terrific. I'll be thinking of you every minute. When I see you at Christmas, you can show me the video.' How did he know about the video?" Mom asked.

"I think Weezer must have told him. She spoke to him on Sunday. She was very excited about it then. She liked the idea of being able to play a movie of her performance over and over again. She said she was going to show it in school."

"I'd better go and see if I can make her feel better," Mom said.

"No, I'll go," I said. "I'll try and get her to think about who can have the extra ticket."

Weezer had almost cried herself dry by the time I reached her. Her face was red and puffy.

"Cheer up," I said. "You don't look like a Little Swan any more. You look like a Little Turkey." That made her smile.

"Are turkeys red in the face?" she said.

"Redder than Little Swans," I said. "Go wash your face in very cold water. Then we'll figure out who's going to get the extra ticket."

"I decided already," said Weezer. "I'll tell you when I get back from the bathroom."

When she returned, Weezer said: "Can you guess who I've thought of?"

"Mrs. Walsh." (Mrs. Walsh was Weezer's class teacher.)

"No."

"Josie?"

"No."

"Ruth?"

"No."

"I give up," I said.

"Mrs. Posnansky," Weezer announced. I stared at her.

"But why?" I asked. "We hardly know her. We've seen her a couple of times to say hello to, and you carried her groceries home once, but that's it. Won't she think it's strange? Some kid she barely knows offering her a ticket to a dancing show?"

"She does so know me. And she's Russian," said Weezer, as if that explained everything. "She said she loved the ballet. She said it the very first time we spoke to her. After my first class. Don't you remember?" I did remember. Weezer had nearly knocked poor Mrs. Posnansky over. When she said she loved the ballet, she probably meant proper professional dancers. I was sure she didn't mean a lot of little girls who had only just started to learn. But I wasn't going to tell Weezer that.

I said, "Fine. That's a great idea. Let your face get back to normal. Then you can go over to her house and offer her the ticket."

"I can't go by myself," said Weezer. "You have to come with me."

"Why?"

"Because," Weezer said. Her lip was looking a little wobbly. Her eyes shone as though she might start crying again at any moment.

"All right," I said. "I'll come." I like visiting people. And I was curious to see what Mrs. Posnansky's house was like, anyhow. "Let's go down now and tell Mom what we've decided."

Mrs. Posnansky took a long time to come to the door.

"She walks slowly," Weezer explained. "She sometimes has a stick to help her. She told me so." At last, Mrs. Posnansky reached the door and opened it.

"Aah!" she said when she saw us. "Is the little ballerina and her sister. Please to come in." She shuffled off down a long corridor and went into a room. Weezer and I followed her. The house was very dark. The furniture was old-fashioned. Weezer and I sat on a big sofa. There was a glass-fronted cabinet full of ornaments. The drapes were made of dark green velvet. There were photographs on the walls of ladies in long dresses and men in furry hats. Some of the ladies had babies on their laps. The babies were wrapped in lacy shawls.

"Please," said Mrs. Posnansky, "you will drink the tea. I fetch. Please to wait."

Mrs. Posnansky brought the tea in on a silver tray. There were lemon slices in the tea, and no milk. We drank it from tall glasses that had gold-painted rims. Each glass had its own silver holder, so that we could pick them up without burning our hands.

"Now," said Mrs. Posnansky. "I find chocolate." She hunted around in another cabinet. This one was made of dark wood, carved into patterns of flowers and fruit. At last, she found a long, flat box.

"Is called 'Langues de Chat,'" she said. "Tongues of cats. I love when I am little girl." The chocolates were long and thin, and lay in a row in their box, packed in crinkly brown paper.

"Thank you," said Weezer as she took one. "They look delicious." Then she went on, "I know you like the ballet, so would you like to come and see me dance on Saturday night? I'm one of the Little Swans in the Dance of the Little Swans. I've brought you a ticket."

"Oh!" Mrs. Posnansky clapped her hands. "Is most marvelous! How you are kind, to think of me. I love to come. Yes, please. Thank you million times. My mother was dancer. I will show. Come."

She beckoned to me and Weezer and pointed
to a photograph quite high up on the wall.

"This is Mother in corps de ballet. In Paris. In
Giselle. Is nearly same as you, no?"

"Wow!" said Weezer. "That's fantastic. A real ballet dancer. Oh, I'm so happy you're coming to my show, Mrs. Posnansky."

"You come one day," said Mrs. Posnansky, "and I show you all old photographs. Is most interesting."

"That'll be great," I said, "but we should go now. My mother says she'll pick you up in the car on Saturday to go to Weezer's show, and bring you back afterwards."

"Thank you, thank you, my girls," said Mrs. Posnansky. "I am most exciting." She walked us all the way to the front door and held it open. She waved at us till we'd closed the door of our own house.

"She didn't mean she was exciting," I said to Weezer. "She meant she was excited."

"I knew that," Weezer snapped. "You don't need to tell me. I always know exactly what she means."

 *Chapter Six*

On the night before the show, Weezer came over to my bed. She shook me till I woke up.

"I can't sleep, Annie," she said. "I'm nervous."

"No, you are not," I said. "All ballerinas are good sleepers. Everybody knows that."

"You're making it up."

"I am not. It's true." It wasn't true. I *was* making it up. Still, it seemed to work. Weezer went back to bed. I thought she'd fallen asleep. Then I heard her say, "I'm nervous, Annie. What if I forget the steps? What if I fall over? What if my dress gets torn? What if—?"

"Stop!" I said. "You'll be just fine. I know you will. You have to be a bit nervous. If you're quite calm, you won't do your best."

"Is that true?" Weezer asked. She was sounding sleepy.

"Sure," I said firmly. "All dancers are nervous before a performance."

"That's okay then," Weezer said, but she was asleep before she'd finished speaking.

"Dancers are nervous," I said, "and dancers' sisters are exhausted." Weezer was breathing noisily by now, and I was wide awake. I fell asleep counting swans.

On Saturday, Weezer said she was too nervous to eat breakfast. She wanted to be the first person in the theater for the show.

"You can take me, Annie. You can help me dress."

"Go on, Annie," said Mom. "Take her good and early. Otherwise she'll drive us crazy with her nagging."

"Please don't be late," Weezer said as we left. "The people who get there first have the best seats. And please tell Mrs. Posnansky when she has to be ready."

"Yes, honey," said Mom. "You go with Annie.

Let me worry about Mrs. Posnansky and where we'll sit."

Weezer must have been even more scared than I thought. All the way to Fairvale High School, she didn't say a word. She held her pink suitcase tight and looked down at her feet.

When Weezer and I are old enough, Fairvale High is where we'll go to school. Miss Matting puts on her show there every year. The school has its own theater. There are real stage lights. The curtains are blue velvet, and there are two large dressing rooms. The girls share one and the boys share the other.

"Look," said Weezer as we went into the girls' dressing room. "See these lightbulbs around the mirror? They're just like the ones in a real theater. Aren't they?"

"Yes," I said. "Terrific. Find a nice spot to put your things, and I'll help you with your make-up. Is your costume on the rail here?"

"Don't touch the costumes," Weezer cried. "Miss Matting said no one was to touch the costumes till she gets here."

"I'm not touching," I said. "I'm just looking. These are the swan ones, right?" I pointed at some gauzy white material. Weezer nodded.

"Yes, those white ones are for the swans. The other stuff is for the girls in the advanced classes. They're clowns, and flowers, and also bluebirds, I think."

"Wow! How many girls are going to be changing in here?"

"About fifty," said Weezer. "But not all at the same time. Our class is first. When we've finished, the bigger girls come in. They have to wait in one of the classrooms till Miss Matting tells them it's time to get dressed."

Weezer unpacked her suitcase. She lined up her make-up, her brush, and her comb. Then she looked at herself in the mirror. "Do I look tired, Annie? I didn't sleep too well."

"You look fine," I said. "Sit down and I'll do your hair."

Weezer had dressed carefully. She wouldn't have to take anything off over her head. My task was to arrange her hair in one thick braid and twist it around into a bun-shape. Each swan had to wear a white satin headband.

"Make my hair flat," said Weezer. "Use lots of pins to hold the bun."

"Right," I said. "You don't want your hair falling down in front of all those people." I saw Weezer turn pale.

"Don't panic," I said. "I'm kidding. It'll take a lot more than one dance to shake this braid loose."

Then the other dancers arrived. I'd just started smoothing pale green eyeshadow on Weezer's eyelids. She couldn't see her friends but that didn't stop her from talking.

"Hi, Tricia," she said. "Hi, Maisie. Are you nervous? I'm so nervous I couldn't sleep. Could you sleep?"

"I could sleep," said Maisie, "but I couldn't eat. I felt sick. I still feel a bit sick."

"So do I," said Weezer. "And hot. And cold."

"You can't feel hot and cold," I said. "It's impossible."

"No, it's not," said Weezer. "My face feels hot and my feet feel cold. And I think I've forgotten how to dance."

"Hello, ladies," said Miss Matting, coming into the room. "I see you've all settled in. Keep your

things in good order. We don't want everyone
going home with the wrong make-up. Now don't
forget…lots of white powder and pink lips. I
hope no one has brought dark red lipstick."

Elizabeth had.

Miss Matting said: "That's much too dark,
sweetheart. Borrow Louisa's. It's just the right
color." Weezer was pleased.

"When can we put on our costumes, Miss Matting?"

"Wait a while, dear. Everything is clean and stiff now. The tulle will go all limp and floppy if you sit about in it for ages. Now I must go and visit the boys."

The boys were getting ready to perform their snowmen's dance. "I don't know why she's going

to see them," said Sharon. "They're not nervous."

"Maybe they're as nervous as we are," said Tricia. "They just don't like to show it, so they rush about."

"They're nuts," said Dolores. "They won't have any energy left to dance with."

"Yes, they will. They always rush about," said Marion. "They're used to it."

The girls sat on their chairs and passed the time by telling ballet horror stories.

"Once, Margaret's ribbons came undone. She fell over them and broke her ankle," said one girl.

"I heard about a girl who was fine in rehearsal. Then she went on stage and started dancing all the wrong steps," said another.

"Stop!" I said. "You're all nuts. You'll be perfect. You're just nervous. You should go and put your costumes on now."

Weezer grinned. "You sound just like a proper wardrobe mistress."

Someone knocked at the door. "Who's that?" said Maisie. "No one's allowed backstage before the show." There was more knocking.

"Come in," I called. A young man came in. He was holding an enormous box made of pink-and-white striped cardboard.

"Is there a Miss Weezer Blair here?" he said. "I have a delivery for a Miss Weezer Blair from the Blissful Bites Bakery."

"I'm Weezer," said Weezer.

"Then I guess this is for you."

 *Chapter Seven*

"What is it?" asked Tricia.

"Who sent it?" Marion wanted to know.

"Where should I put it?" asked the young man from the bakery.

"There's a table over there," said Weezer, hugging herself. "Who do you think it's from, Annie? And what is it?"

"Open it and have a look," I said. The young man put the box down. Then he almost ran toward the door as a crowd of girls gathered round the table. There was a gold envelope taped to the lid.

"I'm going to read the card first," said Weezer. Nobody said a word.

"It's from Dad," she told us at last. Her smile was the widest I'd ever seen. "He says, 'I know you will be a tremendous success. After the show, please share this cake with all the other swans, big and little. Make sure to give some to Annie and your Mom and anyone else who's around.' Oh, Annie, Dad's sent a cake! Take the lid off and let's see it."

The cake was huge and round. The sides were covered in white frosting. Pale blue frosting over the top of the cake had been shaped into waves and ripples.

"It's a lake," said Weezer. "It's Swan Lake, look! There are the swans…eight of them. And they've put trees all around the water, too. This is the best cake I ever saw. What are the swans made of, Annie? Can you eat them?" I touched one to see.

"No, they're plastic," I said.

"Great!" said Weezer.

While everyone was admiring the cake, she whispered in my ear, "I'm going to give a swan to everyone who's in my dance. And to the understudies. Isn't it lucky they put eight swans on the cake?"

"Very lucky," I said.

Just at that moment, Miss Matting came in.

She said, "Louisa, is that your cake?"

"Yes, Miss Matting."

"How beautiful!" She looked around the dressing room.

"Is everyone ready to go on? Yes, I can see that you are. Good. Now we have a special visitor. I know that you'll all want to hear what this person has to say. Please, everyone, sit down quietly."

For one instant, I thought: maybe it's Dad. Maybe he came, after all. But it wasn't Dad. It was the last person I expected to see backstage.

"Mrs. Posnansky!" Weezer jumped up. "What are you doing here? Why aren't you with Mom?"

"Ssh, dear," said Miss Matting. "Sit down and listen. Children, this is a friend and neighbor of the Blairs'. Her name is Nina Posnansky, and she has a very interesting story to tell."

I hardly recognized Mrs. Posnansky. She usually wore dark, shapeless clothes, but she had put on her best outfit for Weezer's show. It was a purple silk dress. She had a sequined scarf around her neck. She smiled at us. In her hand she held a paper shopping bag.

"Good evening, girls," she said. "My English is

so bad, but you forgive. I come from Russia. My mother was ballet dancer long ago. Her name was Natasha Arlosorovska. Before I am born, she dances in Paris. She dances *Swan Lake* in corps de ballet. This I already tell Weezer and Annie."

Weezer nodded. "That's right. I'm going to Mrs. Posnansky's house to look at her photo albums."

"I bring here one picture," said Mrs. Posnansky. She took a photograph in a silver frame out of her paper bag. "This is my Mama. She does the Dance of the Little Swans. Is second from right."

The girls passed the photograph from hand to hand. Four beautiful dancers stood in front of a backcloth painted with dark trees and a moonlit lake. Their dresses were old-fashioned, but you could see exactly what they were meant to be.

"Imagine!" said Miss Matting. "This photo was taken eighty-four years ago, and yet the dancers look just like our own Little Swans."

"They're beautiful," said Weezer, going up to Mrs. Posnansky and giving her back the photo. "Your mom is the prettiest."

"Wait," said Mrs. Posnansky. "I have for you something very special. You come to see me. You offer me ticket. After you go home, I think. I think a lot. I remember suitcase of Mama. Is under bed. I pull out suitcase. I think, maybe is still there, the special surprise. I look, I look. Is much old clothes, old shoes. Is jewels and scarves. Then I find..." She reached into the paper bag. "The headdress of my mother. This is what I seek for Weezer. This is what I wish to give a new Little Swan."

Weezer's eyes were shining. "Oh, my!" she breathed. "Real feathers! Is this the one your mom is wearing in the picture?"

"Oh, yes, same one," said Mrs. Posnansky.

"And you'll let me wear it for the show?"

"Yes, for the show," said Mrs. Posnansky. "But you keep forever. For gift. Is good luck for the ballet. Come. I put it on."

Weezer ran to Mrs. Posnansky. She flung her arms around her. She hugged her. Weezer hardly ever hugs anybody.

"It's the best gift ever," she said. Mrs. Posnansky arranged the white feathered headdress on Weezer's head. Everyone started clapping. Weezer blushed and smiled.

"Well," said Miss Matting. "I've been putting on shows for years, but this is just the biggest thrill. Thank you so much, Mrs. Posnansky."

"Yes, thank you!" everyone else called out. Mrs. Posnansky turned to leave the room.

"I wish you all wonderful dance," she said, and closed the door behind her.

"I've got to go now, too," I told Weezer. "I have to get to my place before it starts. Good luck, Weezer. You look just like a proper ballerina."

"That's what I feel like," she said, pointing her toe and lifting her arms gracefully into the air. "A really, truly proper one."

Chapter Eight

The auditorium of Fairvale High was full. The parents and brothers and sisters of all the dancers had crowded in to see the show. Mom and Mrs. Posnansky had listened to Weezer. They'd arrived early and found seats in the first row. Mrs. Posnansky's sequined scarf glittered and sparkled. She and Mom were studying the program when I came to sit down.

"Weezer is so happy with your gift," I said to Mrs. Posnansky. "She was nervous before you came, but she's fine now. She says she feels like a real dancer."

"*I'm* not fine," said Mom. "I'm nervous for her. She's so hard on herself—just imagine if she does anything wrong."

"She won't," I said. "She's known every single step for weeks. She thinks of nothing but this dance. She even dreams about it at night."

"Ssh!" said Mrs. Posnansky. "Is beginning. Yes." The auditorium grew darker and darker. A thin line of blue light showed under the velvet curtain. The *Swan Lake* music filled the air. The drapes slid open, and the dance began.

The backcloth was painted with a picture of rocks and trees. Everyone clapped when they

saw it. Then the girls came on as swans. They looked pretty. They danced well.

"They're so cute," Mom whispered to me, and I was just about to agree when I heard the introduction to Weezer's dance.

The four Little Swans came to the front of the stage. The white tulle of their tutus fluffed up like feathers. They started to dance. I couldn't stop watching Weezer. She floated through the music as if she were weightless. She bent and turned as

though she had no bones in her body. The feathered headdress made her carry her head as gracefully as a real swan. I couldn't believe this was my stubborn, moody, uppity little sister. She had become magical up there on the stage under the blue light. I didn't recognize her. I wanted to watch her dancing forever. When the music stopped, I glanced at Mrs. Posnansky. Tears were rolling down her cheeks. She must have felt my eyes on her, because she turned to face me.

"I cry because dancing is so beautiful. Your sister, she is ballerina."

"Yes," I said. "Yes, she is."

After the show, dancers and parents and friends filled the dressing room. It was like a party. Miss Matting cut Dad's cake into tiny pieces so that everyone could have a mouthful. Weezer collected the eight plastic swans and gave them out. All the adults kissed the girls and told them how terrific the show had been and how well they'd danced.

At last it was time to go home. Weezer had packed her suitcase. Mom and Mrs. Posnansky had left already. They were waiting for us in the parking lot. On the way out to the car, I said, "You're still wearing your headdress."

"There's no room in the case," Weezer said. "I don't want it to get crushed."

"Weezer, listen." I felt embarrassed. I wanted to tell her how beautifully she'd danced. I couldn't find the right words. I said, "You were the best Little Swan. Maybe it was the Russian headdress that did it. You looked like you were a real ballet dancer, Weezer."

"Louisa," said Weezer. "I figure I should be called Louisa. Weezer isn't the kind of name a ballet dancer has, right?"

"Right," I said. "Louisa from now on."

Almost as soon as we got home, the phone rang. I answered.

"It's some guy wanting to talk to a person called Weezer," I said. She took the phone out of my hand.

"Is that you, Dad?" she said. "This is Louisa speaking."

About the Author

ADÈLE GERAS, unlike Weezer, has never been a ballerina. "I think I knew, even when I was very young, that I was much better at singing than dancing. But I've always loved *watching* the ballet," she says. "Then I became a writer, and now I have the best of both worlds: I can imagine I'm a ballet dancer, or any other kind of person I'd like to be."

Adèle Geras is the author of many books for children. She lives in England in a big city called Manchester, with her husband, two daughters, and a cat named Mimi.

About the Illustrator

JOHANNA WESTERMAN graduated from Scripps College in Claremont, California, where she majored in studio art. She has illustrated several children's books and lives in Altadena, California.